comMEN sense

comMEN sense

**What I learned from dating Mr. Wrong
that led me to Mr. Right.**

Emme Jackson

ISBN 978-1-105-47291-6

This book is dedicated to my husband and daughter-Without you, I am nothing.

Acknowledgments

I am extremely grateful to everyone who unconditionally gave me the inspiration and support to write and complete this book.

To my editor, your assistance and knowledge have been invaluable.

To my dearest friends, you're encouragement was unwavering and very much appreciated.

To my daughter and son-in-law, you always kept me focused and that made all the difference in me setting my goal and making it happen.

And especially to my husband, who is my very best friend; you have given me such a wonderful life! Thank you for everything and then some. I love you.

Table of Contents

Introduction

"Inside relationships it's important to first understand who's coming into the relationship, and not just your partner. You need to understand yourself first."

– Lisa Nichols;
The Secret

Albert Einstein once said that the definition of insanity is doing the same thing over and over again and expecting a different result. Einstein was talking about people and physics, but he could've just as easily been talking about people and love.

I always think of that definition whenever I hear of a woman who's looking for Mr. Right, but instead is dating a carbon copy of her last Mr. Wrong. As I listen to her story, I am all too familiar with how it usually ends. When the breakup arrives, she'll almost certainly shed a few tears, seek solace from friends, and take a quick look in the mirror—then falls for the next Mr. Wrong just as fast as she fell for this one. I know because I did it myself.

The Mr. Wrong I remember best is the last one. Without intending to, he taught me the most about myself. I was in my twenties and way too impressed by the superficial. Aren't we all? Yet now, when I think of him, I wonder what I was so excited about.

For his sake I'll call him "Alan." He was definitely good looking and he definitely had the right résumé: college graduate, drove an expensive car, owned his own home and had an exciting job. He was in sales, which fit him; he could've sold ice to an Eskimo. He was a smooth talker to the point of being sly —the kind of guy who makes a great first date, but not the kind of guy a woman could count on in the long run. From Alan I learned the difference between the two.

We dated for a couple of years and, in my mind, I took that as a sign that we were serious about each other. I looked for other signs, and thought I found them in the words he said. Later I learned that these meant nothing at all. He knew exactly what to say and when to say it just long enough to keep me hooked. I hung on through the good and the bad—mostly the bad— proving just how right Einstein was. I could've been the poster child for his definition of insanity.

Alan was a "player" with a capital "P". Life was a game, and women were his sport. Alan didn't want a girlfriend; he wanted a woman who would give him what he wanted and would accept what little he was willing to give in return. We argued constantly and several times we broke up, but those separations never lasted. It didn't matter because he saw me as the woman who would always come back.

If I ever saw this for what it really was, I was unwilling to admit it. I was in love with the idea of what I wanted him to be. I stayed with him because I hoped that he would change. So often he would ignore me, be emotionally unavailable while dating other woman behind my back. When I'd find out, I'd question him but he always denied it.

We would argue and argue and he'd say I was making things up. Our fights were so exhausting that I'd just give in. I would start thinking maybe he was right, and the cycle would continue (*yeah, sounds like insanity to me*).

The final breakup came at Christmas. The holidays often teeter between joy and disaster. They did for me that year. Alan and I had made plans to spend the holiday together. The day before Christmas he decided to tell me a little detail he had conveniently left out: he had invited a female "friend" named Lisa to join us. Feeling blindsided, I didn't know what to do. I didn't like the idea but I also didn't feel that I had any other choice but to swallow my pride and accept it.

The day arrived and we were at his place. His family was there and I met Lisa. Immediately I had the feeling that Alan hadn't told me the whole truth. Though I thought of myself as his girlfriend, I soon realized that Alan didn't think of me in quite the same way. I could clearly see that he and Lisa were more than just friends. Their body language told me they shared a history and a bond that was exclusive to them, and off limits to me. His family treated her with such familiarity and affection that I felt I was the only one not privy to their inner circle.

I witnessed everything but like an addict in denial; I didn't accept it, yet. The final straw came when I overheard a chat between Lisa, and Alan's sister, Jennifer.

"I really enjoy having you here spending time with the whole family. I'm wishing for that to become more permanent." Jennifer said.

"Ah, you're so nice, Jen. I really like spending time with your family too. You know I would like for things to become more permanent but you know who has something to do with making that happen." Lisa replied with a wide smile.

"Yeah, I know, and he knows how we all feel about having you as part of our family. I'm hoping to call you my sister-in-law soon."

The two of them laughed and hugged each other as if they were sealing an agreement, while they glanced across the room at Alan. Neither of them seemed to notice or even care that I was there. That was it. I couldn't ignore the writing on the wall any longer.

I didn't make a scene. Like so many women who realize they've been played, I just wanted to leave. With all the strength I could muster, I went up to Alan and told him we needed to talk in private.

We went outside and I told him what I had heard. In typical Alan fashion, he said I was mistaken. *I couldn't possibly trust my own ears to believe what I heard.*

"Once again, you're imagining things," he said. "She's just a good friend of the family."

"No, Alan, she is more than just a good friend. I have good male friends and nobody in my family is hoping they'll be a future-in-law." I could feel the anger welling up inside of me as the words came out of my mouth.

"So, you probably heard wrong. You're taking one conversation and building a whole story around it," he said.

"No, I'm not," I answered. "I can't do this...I know what I heard. I am so finished with *whatever this is.*"

"Stop being so dramatic." he said. "You're overreacting."

"Whatever. I am not doing this anymore. I'm out of here." And I left.

As I drove home I replayed our entire relationship over and over in my mind, and that's when it hit me. I had just spent two-plus years on another Mr. Wrong. The only difference between Alan and the others was that he'd lasted longer. Otherwise it was the same story every time.

I could blame everything on Alan, and all the others. I could say the breakups were always their fault, but where would that get me? They were doing what immature men do: looking for fun and avoiding commitment. They would do or say anything to get what they wanted. Again and again I would ignore my instincts and believe what they'd tell me because I always romanticized the relationship. Again and again each one had let me down. Again and again I was failing to learn from the lessons that had been right in front of me. I was living proof of Einstein's definition.

When I arrived home, I had a long sobering talk with myself. I realized that if I wanted something different, I had to do things differently. Hoping the guy would change wasn't the answer; I needed to change.

It was in that moment that I began the much-needed process of performing what I call a relationship autopsy. Like a coroner, I needed to open up this relationship and see what made it live, and what finally killed it. Nor would I limit myself to my time with Alan. While examining that, I would look at the men who I'd dated before Alan, and see what patterns I could find. Once I did, I came to see my past relationships in a new light, as well as my role and responsibility for their outcomes. I saw many things I had done wrong and more to the point, I learned ways to do things right. In doing this I would recover from my insanity.

It's no surprise to me that at the end of my self-imposed introspection I finally met the man who would become my husband, my Mr. Right. He was not like Alan or any of the other guys I had dated. I was different now, and the right man recognized it.

This book is a guide to help you perform your own relationship autopsy. Each woman will approach this task in her own way, but there are some basics that apply to every relationship. You need to look at your love life with a clinical eye, not blaming anyone, and distancing yourself from hurt and anger. You must be willing to look beyond your behavior, and figure out your motivations. If you've always had a vision of Mr. Right, you look at him from a different perspective. Is the man you're searching for the man you really need? Are you the right woman for him?

Though nothing will educate you better than personal experience, that's not the only teacher we have. If we don't break down our experiences to see how they work, we're setting ourselves up as examples of Einstein's notion of insanity. We are asking for more of the same pain.

If you're serious about finding real love, I believe this book can help you. I've been exactly where you are and by reworking my approach I was able to finally attract the right man for me.

It's really not rocket science; the secret to attracting Mr. Right is being the kind of woman he would recognize. Exactly what you're looking for in him, he's looking for the same things in you. It's really that simple.

When you understand that a woman who respects, cares and loves herself is what's most attractive to the Mr. Right's of the world, then the doors that were previously closed to you will begin to open and the right kind of man will walk through asking, "I've been looking for you. Where have you been all my life?"

If you're a woman who has been looking for Mr. Right but instead keeps choosing Mr. Wrong; this is your opportunity to re-write your script.

May you have abundant love & happiness!

--Emme J.

Chapter One

Ready for a change

"As you become more clear about who you really are, you'll be better able to decide what is best for you the first time around."

–Oprah Winfrey

An old Buddhist proverb goes: "When the student is ready, the teacher will appear." In many ways that's how it is with relationships. We tend to think of teachers as helpful, positive people, but sometimes the most effective teachers are the people who give us the most trouble. That's how it was with Alan. Because he turned out to be an almost perfect Mr. Wrong, he showed me what I needed to do to find Mr. Right.

I thought about this not long ago when my friend, Jackie, visited, bringing along her friend, Susan. We were outside when she saw my husband, Greg, through the window.

"You're so lucky," Susan said. "I hate being single. It's not easy finding the right man. Does your husband have any single friends that he could introduce me to? I'm ready to find the right man for me."

"Well what's the right kind of man for you?" I asked.

Susan smiled. "Well, you know… He's got to be good looking; I mean I've got to be attracted to him…"

"Yeah, you got that right!" Jackie said with a laugh.

Susan chuckled in agreement and said "Okay, okay, but he has to be in pretty good shape. No beer bellies! And he needs to have a job. I don't need some guy who tries to live off me."

"I hear you, I hear you," I said. "What woman would want a guy who couldn't support himself? But really, looks, great physique... those are pretty subjective, and they can change a lot over time."

They both nodded. "Still," Susan said, "I'd like a guy who is tall, at least taller than me, has nice teeth and a full head of hair. You know a real handsome man."

"Sure, those things are nice," I said, "but wouldn't it be enough to find a guy who's healthy? If he's basically healthy, but could stand to lose a few pounds maybe you can get him to exercise, eat right... help him get into shape. After all, you can't expect him to be everything you want the minute you meet him, right?"

Later that evening, when I thought about our conversation, I realized all three of us were looking at the situation from the wrong angle. While asking her questions, Susan was avoiding the question that really mattered. Instead our questions were all parts of the question women always think of. It's a question I probably asked myself back before Alan. Whenever a woman thinks about men, she often envisions the right man for her has the combination of all the qualities she wants, and is free of any attitudes and habits she doesn't want. I'd like to think most women are sensible enough to know this mental picture is unrealistic, but still we use the ideal (*as unrealistic as it may be*) as a point of comparison. We have that perfect model in our mind when we ask: "Who is the right man for me?"

It's an important question, but if we let it stand by itself, it's incomplete. Along with it a woman should ask herself: "What do I need to do to attract my ideal man?" Yet, few of us do. A woman who ignores this question is hiding from her own best interests. She wants to find Mr. Right, but she's not paying any attention to whether she is Ms. Right. She needs to look at herself: who she is, and what she does. Before you can expect a man to do right by you, you must do right for yourself and this begins with respect.

The most essential quality in any good relationship is respect. A woman might be attracted to a man with similar interests. She might see traits that complement hers, or aspects of his personality that are totally opposite from her own. Those things matter, but they play out differently in every relationship. That's not true of respect. It's the one ingredient that's always necessary. First and foremost a man must respect you, and he must be the kind of man you respect.

This respect must be a basic quality on both sides of the relationship. It can be encouraged and nurtured, but you can't make it appear out of thin air. When first getting to know a man, respect and appreciation for others, and particularly for women, must be a basic part of who he is. As the two of you get to know one another his respect should grow and evolve. He should come to respect you as an individual, and you should gain the same personal respect for him.

In the course of getting to know one another both of you will almost certainly change. You should be ready for this, accepting the idea that if two people are going to be together, they have to adjust to one another. Sometimes these adjustments aren't easy, but if they are rooted in mutual respect, they will deepen your feelings for one another. If you change for him, and he doesn't meet you halfway, then you've disrespected yourself. You should think of that as a warning, and tell him that things aren't right. If he doesn't correct the problem, and disrespect becomes a pattern, you shouldn't waste any more time on him. Once you've recognized that a man's disregard for you is not going to change, every moment you continue to spend with him is an act of disrespect for yourself.

Respect must be genuine. He can express it in words, but if those aren't backed up by the real thing, then his show of respect is actually an act of deception. That's what I got with Alan. Look at the man you're dating. Are his words respectful? Do his actions match his words? The only way he can show real respect is through action.

Was Susan aware of this? Did she understand that one of the keys to finding the right man is to look inward; asking herself is she the right woman? This isn't a matter of becoming what he wants you to be. It's becoming the woman you want to be, and finding your respect for yourself.

If your relationships have been one disaster after another, then some things have to change. Otherwise you're just asking for more disaster. Until you are ready to change, nothing will change. I had to look at what I was doing. Not only did I have to ask myself the hard questions; I had to answer them honestly. Why did one man after another disappoint me? Why did they betray me? Why did I let them lie to me again and again? Were they at fault? Yes. Was I at fault?

The answer to that was another resounding "*yes.*" The men I'd dated were immature. It was as if they were still in grade school, and women, to them, were toys they played with during recess. I had to face that fact if I wanted to stop dealing with immature men and find a grown man.

If you have an experience like the one I had with Alan, when it's over you can go one of two ways. You can go down the path of insanity, and search for another Alan, or you can decide to change. If you choose to change, then you have some work ahead. That was the biggest difference between Alan, and the men who'd preceded him. When I walked away from Alan I was finally ready to work.

I had the good sense to admit to myself that I didn't want to date for a while. I didn't put a time frame on this. I simply put it on pause, figuring that I would re-enter the dating world only when I was ready and I knew in my gut that I would only be ready when I understood what had gone wrong with Alan, and with others who'd come before him.

There is an old adage in the self-help field: you can't fix what you don't acknowledge. I came to see that I'd spent most of my life avoiding acknowledgement of what men like Alan bring out in women like me. I wanted the man with good looks, a good job, and plenty of nice possessions—the kind of man most women are always seeking. To get him I'd been willing to turn a blind eye to cheating and lies. If a man told me he loved me, I believed him. If I had evidence that he was lying, or seeing other women, I believed his denials. If he stood me up, or took me for granted, I asked why, and believed his explanations. Ever since I was young I'd believe what men said, and ignored what they did. I'd become the perfect enabler for men's bad behavior.

The poet, Maya Angelou has said: "When a man tells you who he is, believe him." To that I would add: "Believe what he says with his actions." Alan and men like him did what they did only because women like me foolishly believed their every word. Such men see love and sex as a game. The Alan's of the world see women as pawns, conquests, and goals in their game. We are the game's equipment, we are the field, and we are the points on the scoreboard. As in every sport, the only real foul occurs when the man gets caught doing something that's against the rules. At that point he gives his defense, and if the ruling goes against him, he pays the penalty, then goes on to see what he can get away with next.

A man's words might be meaningful, but only if they match his actions. If a man says he loves you, defends you in difficult situations, and gives you tenderness when you most need it, then you should believe him. If he has never said he loves you, but he is always there, always supportive, and if he's honest with you even when what he has to say is uncomfortable, then his actions tell you most of what you need to know about his feelings. But if a man professes love and faithfulness, yet time after time he sees other women, and treats you as a plaything, ignore what he's saying to you and believe what he does. His actions are the deepest expression of his feelings for you. This man is telling you everything about himself without saying a word, that what he truly feels is in his actions. A man who does wrong, and always lies about it, doesn't really love you. He's amused by you. To him you are a hobby. He doesn't give you the one thing that lies at the foundation of any healthy relationship: respect.

That was something that I discovered early in my relationship autopsy. As I came to see my relationships as reruns of the same old story (*remembering what Einstein had said about the definition of insanity would have helped*), I recognized respect or the lack thereof as an issue common to all of them. I had never demanded the respect of men, and I had often lacked respect for myself. Women who don't respect themselves are magnets for men like Alan.

To be disrespected by a man you care about is bad enough. What's worse is when you don't acknowledge it. Time and again I'd refused to admit to myself that Alan often acted in total disregard of my feelings. Too many times I'd listened to his lies, and given him every benefit of the doubt. If he came up with an excuse, I believed him. If the excuses made little sense, I ignored that. In failing to hold Alan accountable for his lies, I practically invited or better yet probably encouraged his disrespect. When you suspect a man of dishonesty, you have a responsibility to yourself to ask questions. The same responsibility should force you to pay attention to his answers, and if they aren't consistent, point this out. Some men will pile one lie on top of another, assuming that eventually you'll stop asking. This kind of behavior—particularly if it's repeated—is more than reason enough to end a relationship.

Deception and infidelity lie at the heart of most disrespect. Men like Alan want complete freedom to do whatever they want whenever they want. They usually avoid commitment, or, when they do "commit" their promises are nothing but empty words. Some men feel that avoiding commitment is the right thing to do because they believe that's what men do. This type of attitude is simply selfishness. This man is telling you who he is—in plain language— and as Maya Angelou says, you should believe him. Nonetheless, when faced with such a man, many of us still hear only what we want to hear—especially if he's attractive in other ways. When the good-looking, thoughtless man tells us he's not going to be around for long we must listen. If he doesn't address commitment issues in so many words, listen to what he does say. Does he ever say: "I'll be there for you" or does he even call you his "girlfriend"? A self-absorbed man often deletes words of commitment from his vocabulary. He won't say "girlfriend." Even the word "relationship" has a hard time escaping his lips. He'll see you as a friend-with-benefits, and nothing more.

This type of juvenile mindset guards a man against any threat to his freedom. If he doesn't even utter the words of commitment, then his purpose is clear, he's in it for fun and pleasure, and nothing more.

A self respecting woman would ask more of a man, and a self respecting woman will know what to do if it's not forthcoming. But even a self respecting woman would find it hard to accept. That's when you have to pay close attention to what a man is saying, whether it's with actions or with words.

A point comes where you want something more than a weekend fling. You want depth to match the passion, and you want your investment of time and emotion to be repaid in loyalty and devotion. In other words, you want what the Alan's of the world can never give: true commitment. There are men who will reveal this in plain English; whether it's by using words or actions intended to mislead you and then there are men who genuinely want to commit. So how do you tell the difference between the imposters and the real thing? That begins with you.

Before you can truly recognize and agree to commitment you must be honest with yourself about what it means to you. It comes in many forms, strengths, and varieties, but at the core of any commitment is trust. Both of you must share an understanding of the nature of your commitment. Naturally it's something that will change and evolve, but it must be real from the start. Once dishonesty enters into the mix the relationship or the potential for one is in jeopardy. If it isn't rooted out quickly then the relationship is pretty much over. You both might keep up appearances with your friends, and even with each other, but that only makes you both complicit in the deception. At that point you've joined him in his disrespect for you.

If you are truly honest with yourself you will see this. When you meet a new man you should always observe him. No matter how attractive he is, you should start comparing his words to his actions right away. Look at each situation in its entirety. Look at how he interacts with others. Does he flirt with other women in your presence? Does his attitude toward you change in different settings, and with different people? Be aware of inconsistent behavior and don't be afraid to ask him about it. See if his explanations add up. If you suspect dishonesty ask more questions, and carefully evaluate his answers against what makes sense. Accept what he says as long as it fits sensibly into what you already know. If it doesn't, tell him, and give him a chance to explain. That doesn't mean you have to think everything he says is a lie. You should ask the questions, and then listen carefully to his answers. If his explanation seems like something out of the *Twilight Zone*, then it's time to ignore what he says and look solely at his actions. It's been said that if something doesn't make sense, it's usually not true and once you reach that point you've got to know that if a man tells a lie, then his real goal is to deceive you. If he's comfortable lying to you, his actions won't change anything.

In the spirit of open and honest communication he shouldn't have a problem with your asking questions. Encourage him to do the same with you. If he manipulates this opportunity by suspecting everything you say, and finding fault with everything you do, then let him go. Recognize the sign that's being shown. The sign that's telling you he's the kind of man who sees your honesty only as a tool that he can use to control you, pure and simple.

Chapter Two

You reflect what you are

"The people we are in relationship with are always a mirror, reflecting our own beliefs, and simultaneously we are mirrors, reflecting their beliefs. So, relationship is one of the most powerful tools for growth. If we look honestly at our relationships, we can see so much about how we have created them."

–Shakti Gawain

If all of this sounds time-consuming, that's because it is. If you are dating men in a search for Mr. Right, then you are looking for long-term commitment. Marriage, children, and till-death-do-us-part are the goals here. Those will take up all the time you have left in your life, so the time spent on finding the right partner should be a good investment.

With some men it might be easy. Once you begin to deal with issues of self-respect, and once you start requiring respect from others, many men will rule themselves out in no time. Like, Susan (and almost everyone), you'll still be attracted to good looks. You'll still see a good job, a nice car, and a home as plusses. But the man who has those things won't automatically turn into Mr. Right in your mind. You'll be more accustomed to examining the information against what makes sense. If you see him ignore or mistreat someone, even in a small way, you'll pay more attention. If you spend a half hour with him, and in that time he displays contradictions, inconsistencies or outright trickery, you'll recognize those for what they are. In this way you'll filter out men who normally would've wasted your nights, weekends, months or even years.

Observe a man before you actually go out with him, and then remain observant while you're on the date. How does he treat you when the two of you are alone? What about in front of others? How does he interact with other people? Is he too eager? Is he phony? Is he consistent? Most men reveal their true colors quickly in commonplace interactions with others. If he's Mr. Wrong (*or even Mr. Not-So-Right*) he'll show his disqualifications while the evening is still young. Or he might pass every initial test, and seem even more attractive than before. That's when your investment in time really begins.

If a man makes it to the end of the first date, then what comes next? One thing that's always a gamble is spending the night with him. The timeworn advice about not having sex on the first date is very wise and like it or not, it's spot on. This is when a woman should wait, and it is also when her investment in time starts getting difficult Sex on the first date has always been an issue between men and women. Not always, but often men routinely press for it and women tend to resist. But it might also be argued that sex on the first date happens often enough that it's a routine all by itself.

Every influential person in your life from mothers, fathers, your priest, your pastor will almost always say the same thing: don't do it. Each of these people will have their reasons. But a couple on their first date can also come up with their own reasons as to why it's no longer such a taboo and why it often seems to boil down to one thought: It just feels right.

Okay, it's true that it often will feel right, and in some cases there will come a moment when it is right—but that moment won't be on the first date. For the simple fact you don't know each other, yet. You should want to wait. Aside from the obvious complications like pregnancy and the threat of contracting an STD, traditionally sex has been one more litmus test for respect.

Even if a man tells you its okay, he'll still respect you in the morning, if you have good sense, you shouldn't believe him. Women see sex differently than men. Men see sex as physical gratification. This is their basic hardwiring. A man always starts with the physical: physical desire, and physical satisfaction. Whatever emotions he feels begin with that physicality. Women see sex as an emotional connection leading to commitment and the act of sex is an essential step in the process. If it isn't love in itself, it should imply a potential for love. Men know this. Some know it consciously, some unconsciously, but the awareness is there. Some men learn to believe in, and respect the emotional commitment inherent in sex. Other men think of it as one more female characteristic they can exploit. A real man who believes in emotional commitment will have doubts about a woman who wants sex right away. The man who doesn't will either not care, or assume he has a willing partner who asks for nothing beyond physical gratification. In relationships between men and women this will always be true.

So when is it okay to sleep with him? The reality is it's your decision but if you're really serious about attracting the right guy the honest answer is not until you've gotten to know him well enough to trust him and this will take time. Realize that from the moment you have sex with him both of you will see things differently. You will feel the commitment in yourself, and consciously or subconsciously you will expect the same from him. It's in your DNA. His DNA is different. The act of sex in itself won't necessarily make any difference at all in his feelings for you. If his feelings for you were strong and true they will remain that way. Sex might add to their intensity, and bring out a man's passion, but it doesn't change the depth of his commitment. If it wasn't there before, sex won't make it happen. Sex for the sake of sex is plain and simple lust not love. Men don't confuse the two and you shouldn't either.

In most cases on the first date you don't know that much about one another. Even if you do know one another, having sex too soon changes the equation. From the moment you make the date you are seeing each other from a different viewpoint. In some essential ways you are just getting to know each other. This isn't the time to think of this as a real commitment. This is why you must wait. Maybe he won't like that, and maybe he'll regard it as a deal breaker. If so, then the time you're investing in this guy just got shortened and that's a good thing because that gives you more time for the next one.

But if he's willing to wait, and if you like him, then waiting is a first step toward trust. Trust is the only sensible foundation for commitment. So when can you trust him? When he's proved himself worthy of it, and that can only happen when he's been tested. The tests I'm speaking of have nothing to do with academics but with the day to day frustrations of life. Ordinary frustrations are a basic part of life but you can learn a lot about a man from how he deals with them. If you go out to dinner, how does he react to the wait for a table, or a botched order? When you talk, is he interested in your life as well as his own? If the relationship has progressed, and you call him with a problem, does he try to help? Does he give you emotional support? Is he clueless? Is he angry? Or simply annoyed by your distress?

Time is an essential part in any measurement of commitment. You should look for consistency, and that can only be seen over time. A man might appear helpful, thoughtful and considerate on the first date, easily smoothing over any difficult situations, then, on the second date he could turn tense and obnoxious for no apparent reason. At that point you'll be glad you didn't have sex on that first date.

When you meet a person you see whatever they're showing at that moment. Even over several dates, you may learn something about the guy, but you should recognize that he's not showing you everything. If you see him over a couple of months you'll have more to observe, but a couple of months doesn't make a lifetime.

I'd been dating my husband for several months when I had a small crisis that showed me a lot about him. Self-reliance is a basic part of my personality. When a problem comes up my first instinct is to try and solve it myself. As long it's a situation that one person can handle my independent approach has worked just fine, but when my cars engine started making weird noises that I hadn't heard before, I knew that it was something serious.

Through the early months of our relationship, life was unproblematic. Handling the day to day was just fine until a few things started to pile up and I began to feel overwhelmed and anxious which only seemed to intensify the situation. When my cars engine started making explosive sounds and it looked as though it was going to be a really expensive problem, the anxiety of how much it would potentially cost pushed me over the edge. I knew I needed help and that's when I set my pride aside and I called my future husband. When he reacted to my emotional storm with calmness and understanding, I could feel my tension ease. He didn't have all the answers in that phone call, but he did soothe me and helped me to focus and gain perspective. At the end of the day, he showed me that he was there for me. From that moment I was sure of him in ways that I hadn't before. I knew I could trust him to be there for me.

Over time you will see the principles I'm describing play out. If he respects you, you will see it. If he cheats on you, you will probably detect it. If he has habits or idiosyncrasies you can't stand, you will come face-to-face with them. All of these things will help you learn whether you can trust him to be the man you need him to be, and that's the real proof of whether he's Mr. Right.

Chapter Three

Actions speak louder than words

"It is rewarding to find someone you like, but it is essential to like yourself. It is quickening to recognize that someone is a good and decent human being, but it is indispensable to view yourself as acceptable. It is a delight to discover people who are worthy of respect and admiration and love, but it is vital to believe yourself deserving of these things."

–Jo Coudert

At first some of the principles about dating might seem contradictory. I've noted Maya Angelou's sage advice about believing a man when he tells you who he is. To that I added: he'll tell you through his actions. But what about that first date? If he says and does all the right things, then shouldn't you believe him? And if he's perfect in every way, why not sleep with him?

When two principles seem to contradict one another, the conflict can usually be resolved by searching deeper. The principles aren't separate rules that neatly apply to every circumstance. They are useful ideas about life, which is often unpredictable.

When you're out on a first date you might begin to believe what you see in a man, but that first step should be limited. You should accept what you see, knowing that you will compare it to what comes later. That's when the principle of seeing a man over time comes into play. On a first date most people want to show their best side. If a man isn't at his best on the first date, then you can fall back on Maya Angelou's idea: He's showing you who he is, so you better believe him.

Long after Alan and I broke up, when I'd begun dating again, a man asked me out to dinner. We went to a busy restaurant, and that particular evening they were understaffed. As soon as we'd been seated it became clear that our waitress was serving more tables than she could handle comfortably. It wasn't the first time I'd seen this situation, and I sympathized with the waitress. She was doing the best she could under the worst circumstances.

My date didn't see it that way. When she finally got to us he spoke to her sharply. As she tried to do her job he took a more aggressive tone, both in his voice, and in body language. He was loud, angry, and seemed to have no clue that this kind of behavior was bound to make things worse, not better.

This is the kind of moment when you don't need to watch a man over time. Instead all you need to do is recognize the context—how the principles fit together. It's a first date, when both of you should be showing your best side. A smart man who has control of himself would be patient. A considerate man would see that the waitress was doing all she could. If he felt the need to make a complaint he would find a way to do it without creating a scene.

When a man's deliberate behavior ruins a first date he's showing you who he is. When he mistreats others he's also mistreating you. On that first date I gave that man all the time he deserved. Intentionally or unintentionally he showed me who he was with both words and actions. Maybe this was as good as it got with him. Maybe I was seeing his best side. I didn't feel any urge to find out for sure. I never went out with him again.

What to do about a man like that is an easy call. You don't waste any more time on him. But even if a man displays patience and consideration, and your first date with him goes well, you should still keep an eye out for red flags. If a man is a great first date, but on the second or third date he shows his true colors, the same rule applies: Walk away. Further into a relationship, when there should be growing commitment, walking away becomes harder, but if you find he's unfaithful, abusive, dishonest, or otherwise disrespectful, believe by his actions what he is telling you about himself.

The differences between Mr. Wrong and Mr. Right are obvious and related. Mr. Right likes himself, Mr. Wrong doesn't. It's a matter of self-esteem. The abusive man who can't control his temper doesn't think much of himself. His inability to understand himself frustrates him. When that frustration morphs into anger he turns that on the outside world. Whoever's around him should watch out. A man with high self-esteem will deal with day-to-day frustrations without giving into anger. He's knows who he is, and at his core he is solid and whole.

The man who was so angry in the restaurant was one of several Mr. Wrongs that I dated after my years of self analysis. Unlike some others, he showed his colors quickly, and I paid attention, recognizing what I saw for what it was. This was the biggest difference between how I'd dated men like Alan, and how I dated men after Alan. I'd learned to identify Mr. Wrong at a much earlier stage, sometimes even on the first date—or even earlier. Sometimes a man shows you enough to judge him by before he asks you out.

When I finally met my husband I carefully observed him, evaluating everything I saw. As one date led to another, and more dates led to a relationship, I saw the same man. His various behaviors sprung from a solid core. He knew who he was, and was comfortable with that. Angry emotions and frustrations were slight, few, and momentary. They weren't glaring factors in an unfinished personality. I liked what I saw, and as he revealed more of himself, I found more to like and love. When things went wrong he didn't change. He remained calm, and dealt with it as a mature person would.

Not every Mr. Right will possess calmness and serenity as personality traits. Your Mr. Right might be impatient, animated, and energetic or he might be the type of guy who takes charge. But if he's truly Mr. Right he will understand his own impatience, and know how to control it. If he's a take-charge kind of guy, he'll recognize the difference between effective guidance and desperate attempts at control. He will know himself. If a man really knows himself, he likes himself, and feels good about who he is. Self-awareness is the foundation of positive self-esteem.

Self-esteem is a two-way street. Mr. Right needs it, but so do you. Just as there's no reason to like a man who doesn't like himself, there's no reason for a man to like you if you're given to self-loathing. You need to know who you are and accept yourself, for good or for bad. If you have issues (*and we all do*) you must learn to see them for what they are. Acknowledging them, and admitting your ownership of them is the first step to effectively dealing with them.

Whether you see dating as a path toward starting a family, or simply as a step toward a permanent relationship, your past affects your future. The one thing most of us share is growing up in a family. We might come from traditional two-parent households, or something non-traditional. Some of us have brothers and sisters, while others are only children. Whatever our backgrounds, nearly all of us have mommy-daddy issues. These are the issues we have to own.

Most of us never completely escape our upbringings, but, if we try we can change our relationship with the past. If you hated your mother but loved your father, or if it's the other way around, you should figure out why. If you come from a family where divorce was a factor, or if you suffered abuse, you need to look at those things, and come to an understanding of their effects on you. Look at the people who raised you. Examine how they did it. Learn from what they did right and what they did wrong. Living with your own upbringing is a huge step toward living happily with yourself. That's healthy self-esteem.

In any self-examination mommy-daddy issues usually get the most attention, but they're not the only factors. We also have to look at who we are, and what we have become beyond the scope of childhood. These other issues might have links to childhood and parents, but as adults we've made them our own. What we need to do is examine them, and admit our ownership of them. Otherwise, as with the mommy-daddy issues, they will own us.

These individual issues aren't always easy to identify, but one way to start is to look at what you would like to change about yourself. Are you easily frustrated and annoyed? Do you have a short fuse? Are you submissive, passive, and willing to be controlled? Do you trust to the point of naïveté? Or might you be calculating and controlling?

Examine yourself, and identify anything that keeps you from being the best you can be. These are your issues. Some may be so deep-seated that you'll never root them out entirely, but if you know they're there, and understand their triggers, you can learn to reduce their effects to a minimum, or even turn them to your advantage. Taking ownership of your issues can help you find Mr. Right by becoming the Ms. Right he's looking for[1].

---

[1] Anyone affected by depression, anxiety or any other symptoms connected with mental health may need to seek professional help.

Chapter Four

The problem with lists

"We are taught you must blame your father, your sisters, your brothers, the school, and the teachers-but never blame yourself. It's never your fault. But it's always your fault, because if you wanted to change you're the one who has got to change."

–Katherine Hepburn

Lists often seem to play a role when a woman is looking to find her Mr. Right. Her friends frequently will suggest the woman make a list of exactly what she's looking for. That's the secret, they'll say. You've got to know what you want to get it, right? I've mentioned the qualities most women look for in a man, and I've also covered some of the deal breakers. Once you start going through these, it may seem like the most logical next step would be to organize, categorize, and list them. Many of us see these lists as helpful. When we look at a man against a pre-determined set of attributes it makes us feel as if we're stepping away from the situation and seeing it more objectively. Makes sense, however I learned the opposite is true. I saw this as an illusion. Relationships aren't logical or quantifiable. People aren't simply collections of attributes and faults. We're a hodgepodge of individual characteristics. Our personalities are as unique as our DNA. A set of general guidelines is essential, but a checklist of particular attributes is a setup for failure.

This is something I figured out during my self-analysis after Alan. I'd always had a long checklist, longer than I knew. Alan had fit it quite well. His good job, nice home, expensive car, and good looks all matched the top qualities on my list. The fact that he seemed to be in charge, and had such a sure, smooth way of talking, made it seem like he must meet other criteria on my list. A man with that kind of authority must be solid to the core, right? That's what I thought. After all, he looked good against those checklists.

When I reflected on this I realized my checklist had only gotten me into trouble. The lists we make are a lot like those made by pilots before a flight. We accept them as measurements that reflect reality. But the reality they reflect is only what's there on the surface.

Unlike the pilot, we seem to always measure for the wrong things. We look at success and financial security, and assume that we're seeing maturity. We see a display of good taste, and assume that it coincides with good judgment. Basing our decisions on appearances is like a pilot who ignores the control tower, and relies on the blue skies and calm winds at takeoff to hold throughout the flight. While the control tower radios information about wind sheer, storm cells, and other dangers, the pilot chooses to ignore this and sees nothing but a perfect day. That kind of pilot won't be a pilot for long.

The other problem is we accept our original assessments, and then move on to other things. If the man does something foolish with his money well into the relationship we pacify ourselves with our knowledge that he owns his own home and holds a responsible, well-paying job. We assume the financial blunder is either a mistake or isn't an error at all. We're sticking with our original conclusions despite new information.

A good pilot checks and rechecks her readings all throughout the flight. That's the key to a happy landing. Ignoring new readings could easily lead to a crash.

Lists encourage us to see men on a superficial level. We immediately assume that what we see is what we get. His having a good job tells us he's responsible. The nice house implies that he's a good risk; after all, the bank thought so. The nice car shows us something about his personality. Depending on the make and model, it might mean that he's adventurous, playful, sensible, or just low key. The good looks and lean physique tells us he's in good health.

If we think these things through we'll realize that there's a deeper level we haven't touched. Why should we bother to explore further? After all, if we've checked "yes" in every box on our list, we won't see any immediate reason for going there. But there is a reason. Dating takes time, and we don't want to spend it on men that are undeserving. If you observe, listen, and maintain an objective mind-set, you will see the clues. Sometimes they're so obvious they practically knock you over.

Once, not long after I started dating again, a friend of a friend asked me out to dinner. I didn't know the man, but my friend vouched for him. Still with my newfound wisdom, I kept my expectations in neutral. When we met at the restaurant I was happily surprised. He was attractive and a great conversationalist. All through dinner we talked about all sorts of things—jobs, friends, interests— with none of the awkward silences that often plague blind dates. Yeah, I liked him. Besides being attractive, he appeared to be smart, and he seemed comfortable with himself. I was really pleased, and if he had asked me out for another date, right then, I would've said yes. Luckily he didn't.

At the end of the meal the waiter brought the check. In traditional fashion, the waiter looked first to the man at the table. My date looked at both waiter and check as if they were from another planet. The waiter then shifted his gaze to me, but my attention was on my date. Sensing that some kind of situation was brewing, the waiter set the check down about halfway between us, and said he'd be back to pick it up.

As the check sat there, I looked to my date. His smile tightened as he glanced at the check, and then shifted his gaze back to me.

"Is there a problem?" I asked feeling his awkwardness.

"No, there's no problem." He said but still not reaching for the check.

Let me just mention here that I'm a little bit old-fashioned about these things. It's not that I assume the man should always pay for everything. I just think that when a man asks a woman out on a date, and there's no mention of money, then it's assumed the man will pay for the date. After all, I was only there at his invitation, right?

At this point I still might've listened to arguments in favor of paying for my own meal, but then we had an exchange that went something like this:

"So how do you want to handle this?" I asked.

Raising an eyebrow, he responded with "I don't know what you mean"

"Well, are you going to pay the check?" I asked.

"Why would you assume that I would pay?" he said

"Because you asked me out, remember?"

"So what's that supposed to mean?" he asked. "I never said I would pay and from our conversation this evening, you seem to be making more money than I do, so really I think you should be happy to cover this."

Okay, wait. What just happened? Did he just say that I should be happy to pay for the date that he invited me to? Yeah, right, that's not going to go down. It was clear I needed to assert myself.

"Look," I said in a firm tone, "You invited me to dinner, and when someone invites you, they're expected to pay. If you had no intention of paying, then you shouldn't have invited me."

The fact is dinner was his idea. My anger wasn't about tradition or gender roles; it was simply about good manners, which evidently I could see he didn't have.

After mumbling something under his breath, he pulled out his wallet and paid the bill. Needless to say, that was all I needed to know about him. I never dated him again.

But you know this man really deserves a thank you. From a single dinner date he showed me who he really was. Was he fun to talk to? Yes. Did he have a good job? Yes. Was he attractive? Yes. But the episode with the check revealed one thing that goes beyond lists: the core of his temperament. His arrogance and selfishness was spilling over. This was a man who expected to be indulged and he was content to sit back and take all that came his way.

If I'd wanted an attractive, well-spoken scrub, he would've been just the guy. Fortunately I'd learned to respect myself more than that. I wasn't in the market for a scrub; been there, done that, not doing that again. No woman ever should be.

Instead of making a list, approach each man with an open mind. Allow him to show himself to you. Try to see the whole of him. If he has some flaws (*and every man will*), does he also have advantages? Do his words match up with his actions? Is he responsible in ways that go beyond the superficial? This isn't a list. These are difficult questions, and they often have complex answers.

The one area where you might have a list involves your own behavior. This is a list of "don'ts". Don't sleep with a man too soon. Don't ever date a man who is already involved. (*No exceptions.*) Don't base your judgment solely on looks (*kind of like don't judge a book by its cover, sound familiar?*). And to repeat the obvious: don't make lists, they'll just get in the way and limit your prospects.

Chapter Five

Gifts and strings

"Some of the biggest challenges in relationships come from the fact that most people enter a relationship in order to get something: they're trying to find someone who's going to make them feel good. In reality, the only way a relationship will last is if you see your relationship as a place that you go to give, and not a place that you go to take."

–Anthony Robbins

When a man pursues a woman, often he'll feel compelled to sweep a woman off her feet; many women expect it. Men are programmed to think that this is the way to show their emotions. With some men the effort is sincere, with others it's not.

The sweep-her-off-her-feet approach usually involves extravagant gifts, romantic weekend getaways, and other costly items. Too often I've seen women enjoy lavish courtships assuming that is how things will remain but only to end up in relationships marked by coldness, distance, and silence. If all your communication is centered on material objects, what are you going to say when the primary subject is emotions?

Expensive gifts aren't that different from inexpensive ones. If you're already certain of a man's feelings for you, he could buy you a luxury car and that still may not seem in appropriate, but if you're not sure and a man is simply trying to get you into bed even flowers might be too much. With any gift you should ask yourself: Is it a sincere expression of his feelings for me? Does it show that he was genuinely thinking about me? Does it mean the same thing to both of us?

A gift should be an expression of his feelings. It shouldn't have strings, and it should be appropriate to the existing relationship between giver and receiver. It might symbolize a change in that relationship, but the change should be a part of a natural progression. A good example of this is an engagement ring. Ideally the ring symbolizes a new and deeper commitment between two people. If that commitment isn't there then the man has the wrong idea, and the woman should not accept the ring. If the man has judged the relationship correctly, then the woman accepts, and both people know exactly what the ring represents.

I've witnessed situations where a man gives a woman diamond earrings upon just meeting her. That kind of gesture is at it's best, impulsive, and at it's worst, foolish. Though there might be incredible chemistry between two people, they haven't had time to create the kind of emotional bond that diamonds imply. At this juncture, an extremely expensive gift seems too presumptuous for whatever the man might want. It's possible that he doesn't see it that way, but if that's true it raises profound questions about his judgment or lack thereof. He might be naïve, desperate, needy or simply doesn't have a clue.

Alan was a good example of a man who knew how to tip the scales of give-and-take to his advantage. He was too egotistical to give a woman diamond earrings upon first meeting her. However, he knew exactly what words to say, to get exactly what he wanted.

Our first months together involved dining in nice restaurants, and trips to tropical destinations. He always seemed to say the right things, made the right moves, and that's all it took to convince me he was sincere.

In hindsight I can see the holes in all of this as clearly as if it were a slice of Swiss cheese. A guy like Alan might spend some money on me, but it was just enough spending designed to impress me without committing or digging too deep a hole in his bank account.

Early on I foolishly ignored a glimpse I had of the real Alan. One night when we entered a nightclub, I checked my coat. It was a fairly expensive leather coat that I'd saved up to buy. When we left, I presented the clerk my ticket, but the coat was nowhere to be found. Someone else had walked off with it. I couldn't believe it. I was angry, disappointed and frantic. I really loved that coat and I wanted it back, but now someone else was wearing it. Recognizing I was distraught, Alan placated me by saying: "Don't worry, babe. I promise to buy you another one tomorrow."

The very next day I was anxious to go to the store to buy a new leather coat, but when I brought it up to Alan, he was coy in answering me. He had plenty of reasons why he couldn't go. The time wasn't right. What if the coat were returned? It might be hard to find that exact coat, he had too many things to do, and he couldn't spend the whole day shopping with me. Slowly it dawned on me that I wasn't getting a new coat after all. He'd only told me that to calm me down. He had no intention of making good on his promise. He wasn't being honest with me.

Alan knew exactly how to take advantage of a naïve and inexperienced woman, and that's exactly what he found in me. He was helped by the fact that I was foolish enough to believe in the idea he was trustworthy.

Not all men are like Alan, but even when an expensive gift is given sincerely it can be problematic. Long before I met Alan, when I was in my late teens, I had met a guy named Jeff. He had a huge crush on me and was not shy in telling me. I was attracted to his good looks, but otherwise I didn't take him seriously. I was very young, inexperienced, and had no idea how to receive or even recognize genuine affection. I proved this when my birthday was approaching, and Jeff gave me an expensive gift. I wanted this designer watch and Jeff knew that and made note of it. He bought the watch and to surprise me, he gave it to me before my birthday.

Jeff gave me the watch because he genuinely cared for me, but I looked at it with panic. Honestly, it scared me. I knew it was an accurate representation of his feelings for me, but I also knew that accepting it would imply that I felt that same way for him and I didn't. His gesture overwhelmed me. It was far too much and way too early. Jeff was a good man, but I didn't know how to appreciate what he was offering. The watch was an honest reflection of Jeff's feelings, and, no doubt, he was trying to sweep me off my feet. He knew that it was exactly what I wanted but what he didn't know was that I didn't have the same feelings for him. It may have been the right gift, but it wasn't the right time, and I wasn't the right woman for him.

Gifts, getaways, and expensive dinners can all be a part of courtship, but the main thing to look for on those early dates is substance. Whatever material things he gives you, a man needs to show you who he really is. Jeff showed me his desire for a commitment early on that I wasn't ready to give nor did I understand. Alan showed me a man whose gifts and gestures were calculated to bring about the results he wanted.

When I met my husband, his gestures and gifts were in perfect sync with how we felt about each other. His way of sweeping me off my feet wasn't fake or forced; his actions and words told me that I was special and that's the greatest gift of all.

Chapter Six

The language of relationships

"However good or bad you feel about your relationship, the person you are with at this moment is the "right" person, because he or she is the mirror of who you are inside."

--Deepak Chopra

Once a relationship gets started both people should expect change. Like any other process, a relationship has stops, starts, regressions, and progressions. It may seem to reach a comfortable plateau of stability, but to be long lasting; a relationship without change is a relationship that is over.

In the early part of a relationship attitudes and behaviors are just beginning to shift, and those changes don't yet go below the surface. More profound changes need time. They may start as small differences that require no more than minor adjustments to this new person or to your new way of thinking, but if they're going to last they have to touch your inner core. On a first date you both might pay more attention to looks, mannerisms, and possessions, but as time goes on, and you see each other more clearly as potential partners and spouses, your concerns go deeper. A man might start thinking seriously about children. A woman might see home and family in a whole new way. A relationship might alter the way you look at your job, your parents, your family, your friends and even your past. Anything is possible.

Often the language of a relationship takes on special importance. A woman might listen carefully to the way a man talks about her. Is she his "date," or is she his "girlfriend?" If he talks about something you've experienced together, does he always mention you separately, or have the two of you become "we?"

Though a man's words may say a lot about him, some of the concern about what he labels you shouldn't be so important. If his descriptions and names for you are negative and insulting, that's unacceptable, but beyond that it's easy to assume too much from the things a man says—or doesn't say.

A woman can easily attach great importance to whether a man calls her his "girlfriend." A first date goes well, a few more dates lead to romance, and possibly sex, and a woman wants verbal signs of commitment. She views the term "girlfriend" as that kind of sign. Many women think this way, but most men don't. Many men see "girlfriend" in the opposite sense. Instead of implying profound commitment, a man might see it as a vague description that describes almost any woman he's with. It could be the girl he just met, or it could be a synonym for "fiancée." An unprincipled man will take advantage of that vagueness, and use the term in whatever way profits him most. A man who truly loves a woman might never use the term at all. Some of us tend to misinterpret either one.

Don't get locked into terminology. If certain terms or phrases offend you, go ahead and say so, but beyond that the key is to listen. Allow a man to express himself freely. Men tend to commit more slowly than women. While they might push for a physical relationship faster, settling into a loving bond takes awhile for a man. Don't scare him off. If he's interested his feelings will build differently, and more slowly than yours.

Many women get caught up with the ends, and ignore the means to get there. You see this when other women observe a new connection between a woman and a man. Two people go out on a first date, and the next day the woman's friends are all telling her: "What a great couple you make. You'll have beautiful children." I know how they feel. The sight of an attractive couple getting to know one another makes a woman feel as if she's seeing the birth of something truly special. But a good-looking couple who just met is not a marriage, and we shouldn't try to make it into one. Once again, deeper relationships take time.

When I was first getting to know my husband we talked on the phone a lot—so much that our early phone conversations were just as much of a basis for our potential relationship as the times when we were together. One evening, when we'd only had gone out three or four times, we were in the middle of one of these phone calls when I said: "I'm really enjoying this. I'm interested to see where it goes."

Those were my words, but what he heard was me saying: "I think we should get married" In the split second of silence that followed I could feel him retreat. His straightforward reply was along the lines of: "Whoa! I'm not ready for this."

If this conversation had happened in my pre-Alan days it would've been different. Back then, the moment a man said anything about the direction of a relationship, I reacted in a way I thought would please him. He wants to back off? Fine, I'll try to give him more room. He wants to get closer? "Great," I would say, "that's what I want too." In those days, whenever I sensed a man changing direction, I acted like a pretzel and did whatever made him happy.

That was no longer true. I'd been through the school of Alan, had taken my sabbatical and allowed the knowledge to sink in. I was no longer the overeager young woman searching for a man's approval. I knew what I'd said, and if he'd heard something else the best thing for me to do was to correct his misunderstanding.

Now, when I sensed his urge to retreat, I responded by saying: "Oh wait a minute, don't you get ahead of yourself. I believe you've misunderstood me. All I was saying was that I enjoy your company and I'm interested in seeing where this goes. That's not a prediction, a premonition or a wish. It's just what I said it was: interest in where this goes. That's all I was saying—nothing more."

He'd heard something I hadn't said, and had never intended to say. Why? A man might assume you're going too fast because other women may have tried to close the deal long before he was ready, or he might fear for his independence, or he might just be naturally suspicious. All of those possibilities could've been factors in my future husband's thinking, but whatever his reasons, it was important that we be on the same page.

If I'd said the same thing to Alan he wouldn't have cared. In that kind of conversation his only aim would've been to come out unscathed. But I never would've said it to Alan. The woman who'd dated Alan lacked confidence, and had only dim notions about self-respect. She would've caved in. The confident, self-respecting woman would've gotten rid of Alan after a date or two, or avoided him altogether. That's who I had become.

The other big difference was my future husband. He was nothing like Alan. I was no longer dating a man who saw me as a convenient pawn. Instead, I was dating a man who respected me, largely because I respected myself. He gave me an honest response. He'd misunderstood me. He was enjoying himself too. Our conversation wasn't about marriage. I knew that. For a brief moment he'd mistakenly thought I didn't. Our responses to this misunderstanding cleared it up. We'd both been interested in seeing where this was going. Our conversation was one step in getting there.

I'd been dating my future husband for a year before I heard him refer to me as his "girlfriend." By the time it happened it hardly mattered. I'd already seen that he was an authentic man who spoke truthfully and sincerely. Over that year I'd grown increasingly confident about him. By the time I heard him call me his girlfriend I was past thinking about it. We both knew where we stood.

As you're getting to know one another, it's best to listen to everything. Sometimes you'll hear only silence, but that's not necessarily bad. A lot of men don't talk much. Words and phrases are important, but remember that some of them might not mean the same thing to him that they mean to you. Always look for his real meaning. When you are talking about emotional issues, work to establish common ground. Bring misunderstandings out in the open. Whenever you have any doubts, ask him what he means. If he misinterprets what you say, point that out, and make sure he understands your real meaning.

Also, don't let yourself get too bogged down in words and their meanings. If you find yourself spending every minute explaining yourself there's something wrong. Some men use differences about language and meaning to control a relationship. Their definitions of words and phrases shift to suit their purposes. A man like that will always be trying to put you on the defensive. Don't fall into this trap. If a man is inconsistent or contradictory in how he defines your relationship, it's often a sign of indecisiveness or blatant deception. Recognize that kind of man is not on the same page as you nor is he interested in being on the same page. Acknowledge that and move on.

Chapter Seven

The apple and the tree

"Cute's good. But cute only lasts for so long, and then it's, Who are you as a person? That's the advice I would give to women. Don't look at the bankbook or the title. Look at the heart. Look at the soul. Look at how the guy treats his mother and what he says about women. How he acts with children he doesn't know. And more important, how does he treat you? You should never feel less than."

– Michelle Obama
Glamour,
Dec. 2009

People are shaped by their families. It's easy to forget this in the dating world. You go out to restaurants or movies, hang out with friends, or maybe have a weekend getaway. Often you're introduced to a man by someone you both know, and you might have other friends in common. You see him in moments of fun and relaxation. You know him in this context. That's fine, but it only shows you one side of him, usually his best side.

His family will tell you more.

A family shows you how the person you're getting to know became the person he is. His mom shows you his baby pictures and then embarrasses him with comical stories of crawling, walking and talking. Does he laugh? Does he strike a mortified pose? Or does he become genuinely agitated and leave the room? How does his family see the roles of men and women? When the football game starts do the men crowd around the TV? Are his mother and sisters always in the kitchen? Is this separation easy and pleasant, allowing everyone their natural roles, or are the women quiet and suffering? Is the air full of tension? Is it full of laughter? Or is it somewhere in between? What's his father like? What's his mother like? Is the man you're dating the eldest? Is he the youngest? Is he the middle child? Are he and his siblings coming back to a house and parents they escaped from, or is this a return to a warm and loving home?

The first question maybe whether you meet them at all. Often people are hesitant to bring a date to a family gathering. With many of us, introducing a date to the family is an important step. It signals that we want to learn how this person might fit into our most personal space. It reveals who we are in ways that we might not like, so most of us don't do it lightly, if at all.

I've described my Christmas visit with Alan, and our subsequent breakup, but we were seeing the meaning of that episode in the context of how a relationship falls to pieces. There's more to it than that.

I'd been going out with Alan for nearly three years when he finally agreed for us to spend a family holiday together. Up until then, when holidays arrived we either went our separate ways, or spent the day together, sans family. I'd briefly met his sister, Jennifer, and one of his cousins, but otherwise I didn't know any of them. When we'd been dating a year, I was curious about his family; when we'd been dating two years it still hadn't happened. Alan never said I couldn't meet them, but he never did anything to bring it about either. The fact that I didn't question this said a lot, but I wasn't paying attention.

In the days leading up to that Christmas visit I focused as much on meeting his family as the holiday. Despite my naïveté, I did know that meeting ones family was a big step. Through most of the days leading up to Christmas I assumed it was a step forward. As I noted in an earlier chapter, I was wrong. I began to sense this the day before my visit. That's when Alan mentioned Lisa for the first time. Though he described her as "an old friend," and added that she was close with his family, something about the way he talked about her got under my skin. This was my subconscious mind trying to tell me something. I did my best to ignore it, concentrating my thoughts on meeting his family. I clung to the hope that this must be a sign that Alan was finally getting serious. When I got there that thought disappeared.

In my desire to bond with Alan's family, Lisa took center stage. Their comfort with her stood in stark contrast to their tolerance of me. Lisa was a dear friend—almost a family member. I was just some girl of Alan's who probably wouldn't make it to the New Year. Lisa was the one they'd invested their hopes in; I was someone they'd barely heard of. With the exception of Jennifer, Alan's immediate family hardly seemed to know who I was. When I left suddenly it's doubtful that most of Alan's relatives even noticed.

Years later I met my future husband, Greg's family. In the nearly two years between meeting Greg and meeting them, I'd been aware that they were there in his life, but I didn't push to meet them. I'd learned patience, and I'd also developed an informed trust in this man. He would introduce me to them when the time was right.

The right time finally arrived when we'd been together for well over a year. He invited me to Thanksgiving dinner. Up till then I'd treated most holidays the same way, making my own plans, and assuming any man in my life would make his. As this holiday season approached I saw no reason for it to be different. Greg and I had been taking it slow, which was fine with me. Still, when he invited me to his cousin's for the traditional holiday get-together, I found myself feeling pleasantly surprised. This time I knew the signal was real and positive, but even then, I didn't get ahead of myself. I didn't take it to mean I was "the one." Instead I simply thought of it as indicating a heightened trust and interest on his part. I felt comfortable with that.

When you meet a man's family, you learn the most about your place in his life right at the start. As I said earlier, Alan's family barely knew who I was. Despite having met his sister and cousin, none of them seemed aware that I existed, or if they did, I was just one of many, interchangeable with a dozen other women Alan had dated. Nothing could've contrasted more sharply with this than my introduction to Greg's family.

My future in-laws are a big family, with plenty of aunts and uncles. Greg's immediate family is small, but he has more than enough cousins to make up for it. I met his cousin, our host, and her immediate family first. This was followed by an endless roster of names along with a cloud of friendly faces. Keeping track of them all was a job in itself, but I got through it.

These people had heard of me. Far from hiding my existence, Greg had told them about me. It was obvious that they'd asked for details. This knowledge mixed with their welcoming manner made me feel right at home.

Later the men went off by themselves and talked about whatever men talk about. I stayed with the women. They laughed, told stories, and gave me a glimpse of the world my future husband had come from.

Greg's cousin then came up to me and said: "You know, a while ago I was thinking about introducing Greg to a friend of mine from work, but when I mentioned it, he said he wasn't interested. I knew you two had just started seeing each other but Greg doesn't tell us all his business and I wanted to find out how serious he was about you, so I played a little trick on him to gauge his reaction. I told him that I have another friend—a guy—who's single, and I asked if he'd mind if I introduced this guy to you. Greg whipped his head around and looked at me and said, very firmly I might add, forget about it, she's not available! You know he never brings women around and to get that type of emotional reaction from him let me know my cousin is love-struck!"

"Oh, really, is that what he said?" I asked smiling. It was the first sign of him marking his territory. When I heard the laughter of all the women around us I understood what it meant: They knew too. I didn't see this as a big breakthrough. Instead it was something better: a confirmation of the connection that was already forming and that I fit in.

What lessons can we take from this? One is patience. Don't expect to meet a man's family immediately. If he wants you to meet them that fast it might be a sign that he's desperate, or that it's a chore he wants to be over and done with. Another lesson is in the families themselves. If you walk in and they seem to already know good things about you, take it as a positive sign. If you've been dating him for any time at all, but his family isn't aware of you, find out why.

While meeting the family can tell you a lot about where you stand, it also shows you plenty about him. Who raised him? What kind of relationships does he have with siblings, cousins, aunts and uncles? Are these people trustworthy? Do they trust him? Do they hide things? Are they open, warm, and welcoming? Do they seem genuine? All of this can reveal the inner man. A man's family can't tell you everything, but they can show you aspects of his life that you won't find anywhere else. Through them you can observe how he's dealt with the longest relationships of his life, and that can be the key to your long-term feelings about him.

Chapter Eight

No such thing as perfection

"Find a guy who calls you beautiful instead of hot, who calls you back when you hang up on him, who will lie under the stars and listen to your heartbeat, or will stay awake just to watch you sleep... wait for the boy who kisses your forehead, who wants to show you off to the world when you are in sweats, who holds your hand in front of his friends, who thinks you're just as pretty without makeup on. One who is constantly reminding you of how much he cares and how lucky he is to have you.... The one who turns to his friends and says, 'that's her.'"

–C. Palahniuk

Since the beginning of time, people have fantasized about a paradise where all is right, and where good times last forever (*think romance novels*). Women imagine that all the men there are gorgeous, sexy, loving and faithful, and all the families in this paradise live in bliss.

Okay, I hate to be the one to tell you this but there is no paradise. That world doesn't exist.

Searching for the perfect man is like searching for a needle in the haystack in the dark. Think about it. If there were such a man, how could he want anything but the perfect woman? If he did choose a flawed woman, he would no longer be perfect. It's one of those impossible paradoxes.

However, despite logic the myth persists. It's been celebrated in fairy tales for thousands of years. It's been idealized in movies, television, and every medium where stories get told. I think of it as the "Ozzie and Harriet" syndrome.

"Ozzie and Harriet" was one of TVs first sitcoms. In a time when Americans had only three TV networks almost everyone watched it. Many viewers believed in the picture it painted. The show portrayed a life so close to the ideal that it was hard to tell the difference. Ozzie Nelson was a pleasant guy who was always a friend to their sons. Harriet Nelson was that astonishingly competent '50s housewife, the kind who wore pearls even when cleaning the kitchen. One of their sons was a talented singer, and the other was a straight-A student. The hardest job for the show's scriptwriters was to create problems big enough to be amusing, but small enough to avoid threatening the foundations of this perfect structure. In the idealized atmosphere of '50s TV, the Nelsons were a family that came directly from heaven.

Though Ozzie and Harriet are long gone, the mindset that created them isn't. There will always be romances and comedies where seemingly perfect people fall in love. These stories always present a problem and then offer a solution that leaves the characters lives more perfect than before. As the final credits roll, all the characters go off into the sunset living happily ever after. People love happy endings!

Let's get real. Life doesn't work that way. We all are to some degree, imperfect. We come from imperfect families, go to imperfect schools, and get imperfect jobs. Many of us compromise our dreams, and adjust our expectations. We make numerous mistakes, and sometimes we are less than honest. We're too short, too tall, too fat, too thin, and too eager to be something other than what we truly are. That's how real life works.

Most of us understand this, and consciously or maybe subconsciously we accept it. When a man meets you for your first date you can probably spot some imperfections right away. It might be his height, or a bulging waistline, or maybe he doesn't dress that well. But if the idea of a prince charming has made a way into our subconscious we still harbor hope. Behind these minor physical imperfections we still want to find the perfect man. Some of us even expect it.

We shouldn't.

Why?

It's impossible. He doesn't exist. There is no such thing as perfection.

That imperfect family of yours may have left you wounded. His family may have left him the same way. Now "wounded" sounds like something traumatic that's given us deep and permanent scars: beatings, lies, and psychological torture. It doesn't have to be to that extreme. Wounded might be no more than an overbearing father, or a mother who has a hard time asserting herself. Maybe the man you're dating has a sibling who's painfully competitive. And perhaps you are painfully shy in a family of shouters. But even if someone comes from a horrible home where trauma and heartache took up permanent residence, that doesn't close off the possibility of a healthy, happy relationship. Hardship can make a person better or worse. It depends entirely on the person and what they learned and do to change it.

When we search for someone to spend our life with, we tend to look for the relationship we already recognize from our own experience. We may not realize we're doing it, but we often recreate similar situations to the ones we knew growing up. An abusive partner often replaces an abusive parent. Someone who grew up as the center of attention in his or her family will probably want more of the same in their adult surroundings. A neglected child often chooses a neglectful spouse. It doesn't have to be this way, but if your childhood was dominated by negativity, having a positive adult relationship might be more of a challenge for you.

I've seen too many relationships that failed because neither partner understood their past. Years ago I knew a woman who started dating a guy who was very giving (possibly too giving) in the material sense. In some ways he was just the man she wanted. She'd always yearned for a guy who would spoil her. It was behavior she'd learned growing up. She'd been raised by a mother who had exerted control by doing all the thinking and talking, while her father, a man of few words, communicated by way of giving material things.

Now, without even being aware of it, she'd found the ideal replacement, or so she thought. Whenever she wanted something— and sometimes even if she didn't—he would buy it for her. Extravagant gifts like jewelry, designer handbags, expensive clothing ---whatever she desired, she got; all she had to do was mention it, and soon it would appear before her.

The man she was dating was a quiet guy, almost to the point of having no voice. When he did open his mouth he spoke softly, as if he was wondering if he was speaking out of turn. He seemed happy to be with a woman who was willing to do the talking for both of them.

For some couples this contrast might be a good balance but with these two it was only an omen of failure.

She never once questioned his lack of communication skills or way a man that she barely knew was willing to shower her with all the lavish gifts from the very beginning. She quickly fell into the habit of accepting all the gifts he gave her and without even realizing it, she grew to depend on the gifts. Eventually they got married and from the first day of their marriage these two had an extremely difficult time communicating. You would think she would've seen this coming but she had ignored all the signs.

She married a man, who just like her father, didn't know how to express himself any other way but through giving material things; and just like her mother, she was a woman who was the talker and always took control. Although her husband loved her, he couldn't open up to her emotionally, and she couldn't stand it. She also didn't give him much reason to want to open up to her. Their talks would often explode into a one sided shouting argument. She would scream as loud as she could, thinking the louder she screamed that would get him to express himself emotionally. She didn't realize that screaming only serves to emasculate a man not to mention it shuts down his emotions even further.

If she'd cared to, she might've understood her husband once she met his family. His dad was a quiet type too. In the old days people would've said the man was "whipped". Today we would describe his wife as "domineering." She ruled him completely, dictating his every move. It was obvious she'd done the same thing to their son.

When the son married, he was recreating his childhood home—a place where men said little, and women called the shots. The marriage only lasted a couple of years, but unlike his parents' union, this one finally disintegrated. Like his father, he let his wife's words roll off of him. Instead of giving answers he just sat there. His wife couldn't bear it. It was as if she was angry with him for allowing her to control him.

When she finally couldn't take it anymore and asked for a separation, he reacted by giving her more gifts. Of course, she got the house, but she also got all kinds of new things to put in it. He replaced all the worn out gifts he'd given her and presented her with new, more expensive gifts. The presents were like apologies for a crime that had never been committed. It didn't work. In the end they divorced. Because they didn't think about and analyze their history, neither of them could escape their past.

One thing we tend to forget is that once we've grown up most of us leave our families. We might still be close to them, but we come to a time when closeness is a choice. We can leave the abusive parent. We can cut off the dishonest brother or sister. We can limit contact, end it, or see our family every day. As an adult we have the opportunity to carve out our own lives, and be all that we can or want to be. Many of us find ways to become independent without much change in our family dynamic. Others find that cutting the cord is the only way to grow and thrive.

Whatever you see when you look at your date, know that it is only the surface. His appearance may or may not reflect what's underneath. What you need to find out is whether this guy—with all his qualities and flaws—is a good match for you. Does he laugh at the same things you do? Does he think the same way about issues of right and wrong? Is he strong and settled? Is he nervous and flighty or a little of both? The most important thing you must learn is: Is he what he seems to be? If his manner is smooth, learn whether it's manufactured or real self-confidence, or a mask worn to hide self-doubt. Does his smile come from the heart, and spread across his whole face? Or does it come from calculation, only touching his lips?

William Shakespeare is quoted with saying: All that glitters is not gold. A more modern way to express his quote would be: Don't buy the car without looking under the hood. In other words, always look beneath the surface. Is this man open or closed? Does he talk easily about his background or does he keep it out of bounds? Over time you can look for other evidence, such as consistency. When he speaks of the past does he tell the same story in the same way, or does he change the facts? Is he truthful about his occupation, and past and present relationships? Or does he tell you what he thinks you should hear?

A large part of dating should be devoted to finding out what you might be getting into. At this point your commitment is limited to the date itself, and you can even break that if you want to. You are there by choice, for the purpose of getting to know this guy better. Does he cooperate? Do you?

As it is with all questions about Mr. Right, you should ask the same things of yourself. Are you honest and forthcoming about your background? Do you alter or sanitize your past? Have you come to terms with your upbringing, or is it a difficult subject?

The first relationships most of us have are with our families. Those experiences shape the way we relate to people for the rest of our lives. If we suffer childhood injuries, we must heal. If youth is a long, pleasant ride, as adults we must learn patience. Though some are more glaring than others, every childhood has its gaps.

When you look at your date don't expect perfection, and don't try to be perfect for him. Show him who you really are, and encourage him to do the same. If two people are honest with each other on the first date, they will both know whether they want a second.

Chapter Nine

Double standards still exist

"If you really put a small value upon yourself, rest assured that the world will not raise your price."

–Unknown

I was watching a reality TV show where a wealthy, good-looking young man had to pick between five young women who wanted to date him. We, the audience, knew that real courtships, and the possibility of marriage, were factors in the situation. The women were all searching for a man for the long haul. The young man was less clear about this, which just made it seem all the more real.

Gradually his decision boiled down to a choice between two of the women. One was cute and down-to-earth, a classic example of the girl-next-door. The other woman was absolutely gorgeous. She had the hair, face and body of a supermodel, and she dressed the part.

The man's friends played a role, advising him constantly. When he made a beeline for the great beauty, they tried to pull him back. "Not her," they said. "This is about finding a woman you can be happy with for the rest of your life. She looks great now, but how far will that get you? You're attracted to her for all the wrong reasons. Why not choose the one who's cute, and whom seems to really like you."

The woman who was simply cute looked on as this wealthy, but shallow young man went after the supermodel of his dreams. The young man hardly gave the cute girl- next- door a thought. Instead he focused all his efforts on the great beauty. He hired a helicopter, and flew her to a mountaintop where an elegant dinner awaited them.

The great beauty was impressed. With her looks she'd probably been on numerous expensive dates, but this man had outdone them all. She let him sweep her off her feet, thinking that all this attention was proof of true love. She was thrilled by his looks, his attentiveness, and, yes, his money. A man who would do all this to win her must be the one, right?

Wrong, unfortunately (*actually this was a blessing in disguise, she just didn't know it*). After their mountaintop date the two wound up sleeping together. For the great beauty, she thought this night of passion sealed the deal on their future. For the wealthy young man he thought of it as a night of intense pleasure (*I think they call this a one night stand*).

From there it got messy. The man didn't call her, and the great beauty felt as if she'd been used and tossed away. Later, when he'd moved on to other women, the young man learned of his earlier date's reaction. When told that she'd expected much more, he seemed shocked. "We were just having a good time", he said. He told his friends how he'd truly enjoyed his night with the great beauty. She'd seemed to enjoy every minute of the evening, but he'd assumed she understood that was all it was. After all, she'd been totally ready to jump into bed with him, having just met him. What did she expect?

The beautiful young woman felt as if she'd been deceived. She'd had placed her hopes in this man. She'd believed his words, his affection, his extravagance, and definitely, his money. She'd sincerely wanted love, but the reality is that his money and wealth had blurred her vision. What probably took her longer to learn was that sex was just as blinding as riches. She'd seen sex as something that united them forever. He'd seen it as a fun night.

We live in a time when we're encouraged to think of sex and love as different things. They are, yet they are not. The physical act of sex is not the same as love, and love is not simply sex with some emotion thrown in. But the two are connected.

The standard advice for the great beauty has been around forever: Don't have sex with him on the first date. Many would add, as I do: Don't have sex with him on any of your early dates or too soon. Wait until you understand with certainty what's going on between you. He's going to think of sex differently than you do. So will your friends. So will your mother. So will society. Though many people won't admit it, almost everyone sees men and sex differently than they do women and sex.

Women and men both want to pretend that sexual double standards have disappeared. They haven't. Attitudes about sex, and its timing, are riddled with myths and false assumptions. The first and foremost myth is: The timing of sex doesn't matter. The immature man wants this to be true because it allows him to have sex without consequences. A woman wants it to be true only when she's hiding from the truth about her feelings—and his.

The second myth about sex is that its consequences are exactly the same for the man as they are for the woman. The first fact to crack this myth is that of basic biology. A woman is hardwired to take sex more seriously. Whether she admits it or not, she usually sees sex as being connected to some degree of commitment. Even if she tells herself that it's all just a part of having a good time, in her heart she feels it's more.

Many men don't see it that way, and that's where the double standard hits home. We live in a culture that doesn't expect men to take sex as seriously as women do. This comes to us in signals from our parents, our teachers, our songs, our movies, and all other media. Men sow wild oats. Women keep their virtue. Men who have sex with a lot of women are called "players." Women who have sex with a lot of men are called "sluts."

These are obvious signs, but more subtle hints play a part. If a man gets a woman to have sex with him quickly, he often begins to lose interest. This isn't because of boredom. He hasn't had time to get bored. It's because he thinks of her as an agent of pleasure, but not as an object of love, or a partner in building a family. To most men, a woman who wants sex right away will always be seen as a one-night stand. That doesn't mean he'll only have sex with her one time. It means that he sees each night they spend together as a separate moment, with no strings attached. He assumes she sees it the same way.

Many women make the mistake of thinking that if she has sex with a man before really knowing him, it will deepen his commitment to her. Such a woman sees sex as a measure of a man's emotional obligation. It's not. That doesn't mean that men keep sex and emotion completely separate, but the emotions men feel about sex are centered more in the moment. The passion they feel is temporary. Any attachment they feel is often compromised by an innate ambivalence. Anything that resembles "love" is fleeting.

This isn't always true. If a man honestly loves a woman sex will become a passionate expression of his love. But before sex and love can connect in a man, the love must already be there. Though these two things complement each other, one doesn't produce the other.

So when is the right time to have sex with a man? It's when you've both advanced beyond the illusions, and found the beginnings of love in each other. You don't do it to deepen that love. Though it's possible for sex to run parallel with deepening affections, when that happens it's a happy accident. You don't do it to attract the man to a greater commitment. He won't see it that way, and if he senses that you do, he's more likely to run than to fall in love.

Sex should come when you feel certain his emotions are in synch with yours. It should be an expression of what's really there between you, not what you hope is there. Sex can be healing, transformative, and ecstatic, but it can only be those things when it's an honest expression of something deeper. Sex can help us focus our love, but it is not love itself.

This isn't to say that sex should only happen in situations that lead to marriage. You're an adult woman, if you can enjoy sex without deep emotional commitment, that's your prerogative; but make sure that's really the case. Examine your feelings and expectations carefully. Do you want this date to turn into a relationship? Does this relationship have a chance to grow? In situations like those, sex should be postponed until you're sure that he's as serious about you as you are about him.

Chapter Ten

Love & Money

If you aren't good at loving yourself, you will have a difficult time loving anyone, since you'll resent the time and energy you give another person that you aren't even giving to yourself. "

–Barbara De Angelis

Is money the root of all evil? Hard to say, but it's been the root of far too many conflicts between men and women. Money, and the things it can and can't buy, is a factor in every long-term relationship. Occasionally two people approach finances in ways so similar that they always find agreement. More often questions come up. How you resolve them can show you a lot about the man you're dating, and about yourself.

On your first date general finance shouldn't be an issue, but that doesn't mean money isn't involved. Most dates have some costs. So if you're looking to the future, the one thing you want to see is that the guy is using money wisely and responsibly. He shouldn't try to buy his way into bed with you, or impress you with expensive gifts. He shouldn't have to communicate his feelings with money or material goods. Even if you have no thought of a more permanent relationship, those principles apply. If the temporary date wants to throw money around, that's fine, but he should be absolutely clear about what he's buying, and he should know that it doesn't include you.

One thing to watch for is gifts on first dates. An inexpensive knick-knack might be fine, but if he arrives at the door with a gift that's extravagant, like a diamond necklace, it would be wise for you not to accept. Even if the guy is rich enough to ignore the cost, he should know that you are not. Just as it's important for you to know how money fits into his world, it's equally important that he understand how it fits into yours. That helps eliminate potential mis-communications.

Another area to watch, even at the beginning, is what might be called "financial etiquette." I've already cited a great example of this in my experience with the date that wouldn't pay for our dinner. If you recall, this was a date that had gone well until the check came. That's when the guy's attitude put a chill on the evening, ending any chance of a second date. Though he'd asked me out on the date, he resisted paying the check. He then went beyond that, and resisted paying anything at all. He expected me to pay for everything. He was attractive, pleasant, and interesting enough, but this behavior was a deal breaker. The principle he was violating was simple and straightforward: If you ask someone to go out with you, it's assumed you pay the bill. Reluctantly, he did, but his sudden shift to grudging resistance led me to write him off. None of us need, and few of us can afford, a freeloader.

This brings us to another red flag: the man who asks for a loan. This is a sure sign of a freeloader. If this happens on a first date, you should stop things right there. Whether you officially end the date on the spot is up to you, but if you're smart, the moment he asks, any potential for further dates should be over.

But what if he asks for the loan on the second date, or the twentieth? The red flag is still there. If there are any exceptions to this rule, they are few and far between. The key to financial behavior is responsibility. As your relationship progresses he should be giving you evidence that he can manage his money with honesty and reasonable competence.

He doesn't have to be rich, and his financial picture doesn't need to be perfect, but he shouldn't be talking about loans, or urging your involvement in any other substantial transactions, unless and until you've both reached the point of transparency: When you open your books to each other.

And when should that be? Not until you're both planning to spend the rest of your lives together. Until then you should keep your finances separate, and he should understand that.

You should never open your financial records to a man who's not doing the same for you. This is just sensible thinking. If there's been no talk of marriage (*aka a proposal and a ring on your finger*), and a man asks to look at your finances, you should challenge him to explain why. In most cases discussion of marriage should predate, or parallel talk about an individual's personal finances.

There's a flipside to this, and what happened to a woman I met shows how poor financial etiquette is not an issue reserved just for the men. Not having a solid grasp on your finances whether you're a man or a woman, can foul up prospects in any relationship.

The woman was very nice and she had made it her goal to get married. She was dating with high expectations that things would lead towards something very promising and that she could actually find and meet the one. Sounds great, right? Yeah except for the fact that she wasn't being completely honest with herself about what she had to offer this potential Mr. Right.

Just as I've shared the story of Alan and how he looked great on paper; but underneath all that glitz, he was actually a complete sham; that's how it was with this woman. Outwardly she appeared to have all that a man would want: beauty, brains and then some but inwardly she was a complete and total mess!

Her biggest issue was her finances and they were a complete disaster. She admittedly would say she was horrible with handling money, she barely knew what was in her checking account on any given day. She was living way beyond her means and frequently she faced eviction and repossession notices. Receiving calls from multiple bill collectors had become such the norm but yet that didn't seem to faze her.

She was overlooking (or maybe in complete denial about) an important quality in attracting Mr. Right and that quality is stability. Just as I've previously written that exactly what a woman is looking for in Mr. Right, it makes sense that he's looking for the same things in her. Starting a relationship rooted in chaos and instability I am certain aren't qualities that a sensible person would willingly choose to attach themselves to.

As a relationship matures, and you talk seriously of marriage, that's when the two of you should reach the mutual decision to open your books to each other. When this happens, you must be absolutely honest, and make sure he is too. If anything looks questionable, ask about it. You should require complete answers, and give them too. If he's hiding anything, or if what's there doesn't match up with what he's led you to believe, there's a very good chance that you've run into a deal breaker.

Some of you might feel this process is far too dry and businesslike. After all, everlasting love shouldn't be affected by money, should it? No, it shouldn't, but the only way to make sure love can grow unhindered is to put on your "big girl" pants and settle your approach to money and possessions, candidly and truthfully. It's a slow process, and not very romantic, but it's as necessary to the life of a relationship as breath is to the life of a human body.

In my own pre-Alan days I seldom gave a man's finances any serious thought. I looked at a man's car, home, and other possessions, and allowed them to impress me. In my post-Alan education my attitudes about this changed. As I realized that I should be looking for more emotional maturity in men, it made sense that I would also demand a more mature approach to money. I would pay more attention to a man's honesty than to his bankroll.

In the early days of dating my future husband, he never told me what he had or how much money he made. In fact, on our first date, he picked me up in one of his cars. He chose the late model car that wasn't flashy; it may even have had a few dents and scratches. I learned later in our courtship that he purposefully did this to find out what type of woman I was. If the appearance of his car mattered to me, he would know that I was the superficial type and that would have been his deal breaker. Fortunately, it didn't because I was no longer that kind of woman. He saw the real me and in return he was comfortable in showing me the real him and all his wealth.

Chapter Eleven

True potential

"When you meet a man, you judge him by his clothes; when you leave, you judge him by his heart."

–Russian Proverb

Some years ago, before I was married, I met a man through a mutual friend. This meeting wasn't intended to be a hook-up or even a real connection. Nonetheless, I was young and single, and when we are young and single we view our social group through a lens that's shaped, at least in part, by the possibility of relationships.

My immediate thought was: I'd never date this guy. He wasn't repulsive or ugly, but there were things about him that didn't vibe with me. The most noticeable one wasn't terribly important. He was short and I wasn't into short men. If his height had been offset by great looks or a charismatic personality, I might've considered an interest in him, but while he wasn't bad looking, he just wasn't my type and there wasn't any chemistry. He was a little bit of a know-it-all, and he amplified that flaw with a loud voice. I was unimpressed.

In the months that followed, I had attended various functions and I would see this guy along with our mutual friend and my initial impression remained the same. If anything, I started to become annoyed just by his presence. It seemed as if I couldn't chat alone with my friend without this guy inserting himself into the conversation. His obnoxiousness grated on me so much that I could barely stomach him.

Several months passed, and I hardly thought of this man at all, then one night our mutual friend invited all his friends to a dinner at a local restaurant. Knowing this guy would be there, I was prepared to be irritated by him but to my surprise he showed up at the dinner with a date.

His date was a very attractive woman but she had a physical deformity that would've challenged anyone's capacity for sensitivity. She had a cleft lip and from their interactions I could see that he accepted her and her handicap without pity, or any other form of judgment or condescension. Besides her beauty, she was very charming and friendly, and that was all that seemed to matter to him. I'm not saying they were a perfect match, but on a dinner date with friends they seemed like a good couple. He was sensitive to her disability without being emotionally overwhelmed by it.

Eventually these two parted, and as I understood from my friend, the guy had moved on, marrying another woman and having children. Some years later I saw photos of this man with his new wife and kids. But now, when I looked at him in the pictures I no longer saw the obnoxious man from before; I saw the undeniable love this man had for his wife and his kids and it was beautiful, it was real. What had I missed way back when I'd first met him? What I had missed was his true potential.

Whenever we look at other people we make judgments about them. Though it's easy to get carried away with this, judging people is both natural and at times necessary. If we're thinking of getting a ride with someone, we want to know if he or she is a safe driver.

When we're sitting at dinner with a date, we watch and listen, judging whether we want another date, or whether this experience might develop into something deeper. When we do that, we're evaluating this person's potential.

When you look at a man with thoughts of the future, potential is all you have. Would he make a good husband for you? Would you be a good wife for him? Would he make a good father? Will he be faithful? Those questions all come from concern about potential. At their core are even more fundamental questions: Is he honest? Is he strong? Does he have courage? Is he faithful? Is he a hard worker or lazy?

These questions are all about the character of a man. Their answers will tell you a lot about what he might become. That's his potential. If a man is always grumpy, don't expect him to become a sunny optimist. If a man is in the habit of lying to cover up his failings, he's not likely to become honest and reliable. If a man has been lazy all his life, he's not likely to develop a solid work ethic overnight. These are all issues involving potential.

Often we misread potential because of looks. We see the well dressed handsome man, and assume he must be successful and very important. If he says the right things with the strong voice of authority, we're inclined to believe everything he says and that's usually when we'll fall for him. But most of the time we shouldn't.

I was attracted to Alan because of looks. I saw his expensive car and his house as evidence of his well-paying job. What I thought I saw was a life of fulfilled potential that seemed ready-and-waiting for me. What I got was an unfaithful man who would use me for as long as I let him.

Alan showed me his ability for potential many times. From the start he showed me that he could charm anyone. In an honest man this would come out as tact, diplomacy and genuine interest. In Alan, all it really showed was a huge ego. He showed me he had the means to provide for a woman, but he never demonstrated that I was the woman he had any interest in providing for. He showed me his truest self one afternoon we spent at a festival. We heard what sounded like a gunshot-like bang that sent everyone running for cover including Alan but he ran away without me. He didn't bother to concern himself with my safety or whether I was okay. That was my very best look at his capacity for potential but, *again*, I wasn't paying attention.

Years later, when my future husband picked me up in his not so flashy car, I was looking for a different kind of potential. Was this man honest? Was he reliable? Was he authentic? Did he have a real capacity for love? Together could we create a real relationship based on honesty, fueled by love, and strong enough to last through good times and bad? After graduating from the school of Alan, I had learned the difference between the emptiness of the superficial versus the real meaning of solid potential. My future husband knew those things too. He picked me up in his unimpressive car simply because he wanted to see what kind of potential I brought to the table. He was evaluating me to see if I was interested in getting to know him or was I only interested in what he had. My getting into his car without saying a word about its appearance signaled to him that we were off to a good start and that I just might be the one.

Chapter Twelve

Lessons learned

"Do you want to meet the love of your life? Look in the mirror."

—Byron Katie

There are many ways of preparing yourself to meet Mr. Right, and an infinite number of paths leading to Mr. Wrong. The main difference between them is confidence. If you've looked carefully at yourself, assessed what's there, and learned ways to improve upon and accentuate the best qualities of who you really are; you stand a much better chance of attracting the right man. If you base your search on superficial qualities, and judge a man on the basis of the immediate gratification he gives you, then you're only looking for trouble.

At the root of confidence is self-esteem. Some people have this naturally, and their confidence is hard to shake, but most of us have to build our confidence slowly, piece by piece. We do it by taking a hard look at ourselves, and learning who we are. We must be honest with ourselves. If you have a fault, admit it. You won't be able to overcome it or change it until you know what it is. You'll find strengths too, and once you find them you can make them work for you. Learn what's good about yourself, and put your positive attributes on display. When you first meet a man you want to be at your best. To do that, you have to know the best things about yourself. They're there. If you don't know what they are, you just have to look for them. Your best qualities are the keys to self-esteem, and by knowing them, confidence will show.

You can't be anyone except your genuine self when looking for the right man and you shouldn't try to be. You are who you are, and you shouldn't change that. In the world of dating it's easy to lose track. You hear about what men want, watch shows about healthy relationships, read books, visit websites, and soon you find yourself following instructions while tweaking this or altering that. You wear your hair differently, change your makeup, and see where those get you. You smile a lot, laugh a lot, and soon you're trapped in a persona that isn't really you. It happens without you even noticing.

When you spend all your time on appearances, you begin to judge others by theirs. You believe in what you see at first glance. First impressions can be accurate, but only if what's beneath matches what's on the surface. All that glitters is not gold, and just as often a dull surface will hide a true gem. I've told the story of one man whose gorgeous looks shrouded a spirit of frivolous selfishness. I allowed him to string me along for years. That led me to my self-analysis. After that I met a man whose values weren't dictated by appearances. I was confident enough in my own values to look below his surface. I didn't have to dig too deeply to realize he was something special. Even better, I was ready for him. My confidence had put down deep roots.

Confidence is the single most important factor. With it you can trust yourself, and your evaluations of others.

Ultimately confidence comes from within, but often it won't emerge without proper nurturing. The best way to nurture confidence is to repeat the actions that produce the results you're seeking. If you do the right things, you will see better results, giving you the confidence to continue. If you make these into habits, you will soon see positive outcomes. That will increase your confidence, which will give you a better chance of attracting the right man.

The best way to know a man is by his actions, not his words. That's not to say you should suspect that everything he'll say will be a lie, but if he says one thing and does another, the truth will be in what he does. If he constantly shows you respect and consideration, then you should believe those things.

The age old wisdom: never judge a book by its cover is true; don't just look at the surface. If a man drives a boring car, or doesn't dress well, don't make snap judgments and allow those things to turn you off right away. If he's not the most attractive man around, but you sense even a spark of chemistry, that shouldn't disqualify him either. If you get past the looks and the car, what's underneath? Is he honest, kind and responsible, or shallow, selfish and mean-spirited? Often these differences aren't as obvious as we might think.

It takes time to get to know anyone. With that in mind, you should avoid sex on the first date. This probably applies to a number of dates. Is there a magic number? No. This instruction isn't exact, and there's no precise formula. There is only a general principle: don't have sex with a man until you really know who he is.

We develop honesty and trust early, almost always in the home. What kind of family did he grow up in? Were they warm, loving people, or was it a cold, cruel, or indifferent atmosphere? Did he escape a sad childhood, or did his family give him confidence? Has he worked through his mommy-daddy issues? A man's friends and family will tell you a lot about him. Sometimes they'll tell you things directly, such as family history, and personal stories. But they'll also say a lot with their actions. Two of the most important questions are: do they trust him? And do you trust them?

Finally, you have to take the questions you ask about him, and turn them on yourself. Have you resolved your issues? Are you honest with the men you date? Are your words and actions honest? Do you have sex with men for all the wrong reasons, and none of the right ones? If he digs below the surface what will he find?

When searching for Mr. Right the first thing to look at is the first thing he will see: you. If you have a low opinion of yourself, why should he disagree? If you can't face your issues, and resolve them, you can't expect him to do it for you. Again, none of us is perfect, but we don't need to be. We simply need to be who we really are. If you work through your problems, and face the world with honesty and confidence, you can find your Mr. Right. Don't be surprised that he may be different than what you expect, but if you search with genuine confidence lighting your way, you will find him there, looking back at you!

www.ingramcontent.com/pod-product-compliance
Lightning Source LLC
Chambersburg PA
CBHW021246280526
45784CB00005B/2257